Theodora the "Believing Queen": A Study in Syriac Historiographical Tradition

Analecta Gorgiana

1040

Series Editor

George Anton Kiraz

Analecta Gorgiana is a collection of long essays and short monographs which are consistently cited by modern scholars but previously difficult to find because of their original appearance in obscure publications. Carefully selected by a team of scholars based on their relevance to modern scholarship, these essays can now be fully utilized by scholars and proudly owned by libraries.

Theodora the "Believing Queen":
A Study in Syriac
Historiographical Tradition

Susan A. Harvey

gorgias press
2011

Gorgias Press LLC, 954 River Road, Piscataway, NJ, 08854, USA

www.gorgiaspress.com

Copyright © 2011 by Gorgias Press LLC

Originally published in 2001

All rights reserved under International and Pan-American Copyright Conventions. No part of this publication may be reproduced, stored in a retrieval system or transmitted in any form or by any means, electronic, mechanical, photocopying, recording, scanning or otherwise without the prior written permission of Gorgias Press LLC.

2011 ܟܒ

ISBN 978-1-4632-0088-6   ISSN 1935-6854

Extract from *Hugoye: Journal of Syriac Studies* 4 (2001)

Printed in the United States of America

THEODORA
THE "BELIEVING QUEEN:"
A STUDY IN SYRIAC
HISTORIOGRAPHICAL
TRADITION

SUSAN A. HARVEY

BROWN UNIVERSITY
DEPARTMENT OF RELIGIOUS STUDIES
PROVIDENCE, RI
USA

ABSTRACT

Syriac tradition remembers the sixth century for the tragic separation of the Eastern and Oriental Orthodox churches. The Byzantine emperor Justinian I is remembered as the harsh persecutor of the faithful, while his wife Theodora is revered as the "believing queen," champion and protectress of the dissenting non-Chalcedonian church. Greek and Syriac sources of the sixth century present more complex views of the imperial couple, with sharply differing portraits of Theodora used to interpret the reign. Later Syriac chronicles rework and reshape the sixth century material, fashioning a significantly changed historical experience for the Syriac Orthodox through a changed memory of Theodora's past.

Remembering Theodora

[1] Students of Byzantine history are generally presented with the sixth century as one of the great eras of all time, due to the extraordinary reign of the Emperor Justinian I ("the Great") and his wife Theodora. Justinian's was a lengthy tenure, technically from 527 until his death in 565, although he is credited with carrying much of the imperial burden during the previous reign of his uncle Justin I, emperor from 518–27. With Justin I, Justinian articulated a vision of a restored and mighty Roman Empire that would reunite west and east politically, through reconquest of lost territories; and theologically, through a resolution of the bitter divisions that had followed the Council of Chalcedon held in 451. Theodora ruled as Justinian's consort and partner until her death in 548, a loss from which Justinian seems never to have recovered.

[2] With Theodora's help, Justinian's efforts touched every branch of imperial life: not simply military campaigns or foreign diplomacy, but law reform, architectural developments, institutional advances in the areas of hospitals and care for the needy, literary achievements, and theological dialogues of the most sophisticated kind. The Justinianic Law Code, the church of Haghia Sophia and other remarkable buildings, the exalted hymnography of the Syrian poet Romanos Melodos—all stand as monuments to the glorious work of Justinian's reign and Theodora's patronage. At the same time, there were spectacular failures: partial and short-lived reconquest of North Africa and Italy, a bankrupt imperial treasury, and a church tragically ripped asunder with the formation of the separated Oriental Orthodox church hierarchies.[1]

[3] In Syriac tradition, this huge panoply is telescoped to a specific focus. The sixth century is remembered as a time of multiple calamities (drought, famine, plague, war), of which the persecution

---

[1] For a general introduction see Robert Browning, *Justinian and Theodora*, rev. ed. (London: Thames and Hudson, 1987). Important assessments of the reign may also be found in Judith Herrin, *The Formation of Christendom* (Princeton: Princeton University Press, 1987) and Averil Cameron, *The Mediterranean World in Late Antiquity, AD 395–600* (New York: Routledge, 1993). For the religious issues, W.H.C. Frend, *The Rise of the Monophysite Movement* (Cambridge: Cambridge University Press, corrected ed. 1979) remains basic.

of those rejecting the Council of Chalcedon and the subsequent separation of the churches proved the lasting tragedy. While it was a long time before the separated hierarchies stabilized into distinct churches (now referred to as the Oriental Orthodox as opposed to the Eastern—or Chalcedonian—Orthodox), the weight of historiographical memory sets the sixth century and the reign of Justinian and Theodora as the determinative point in the process.[2] In the particular shaping that Syriac historiography gave to the experience, Justinian is remembered as the one who caused the separation of the churches through his policy of persecution for all who did not accept the Council of Chalcedon. Theodora, on the other hand, is remembered as the "believing queen," champion and protectress of the dissenting non-Chalcedonian church.

The scale of accomplishment and suffering, of ambitions and loss was enormous, but what lends a romantic glow to the sixth century are the powerful personalities of Justinian and Theodora, towering as tall as their achievements. In western scholarship, study of the sixth century and its most famous imperial couple has relied heavily on the works of the Greek historian Procopius of Caesarea.[3] Procopius was an official chronicler of Justinian's reign and one privy to the imperial court at various levels. Procopius' *History of the Wars*, covering the campaigns against the Vandals, Goths, and Persians, provides our most detailed account of Justinian's military engagements.[4] His work entitled *Buildings* offers a formal and detailed report on the architectural accomplishments,

---

[2] The critical study is E. Honigmann, *Évêques et évêchés monophysites d'Asie antérieure au VIe siècle* (CSCO 127, Sub. 2; Louvain: Secrétariat du CSCO, 1951); cf. also A. Van Roey, "Les débuts de l'église jacobite," in A. Grillmeier and H. Bacht (ed.), *Das Konzil von Chalkedon: Geschichte und Gegenwart* (Würzburg: Echter-Verlag, 1951–4, 1973) Vol. 2, 339–60. For the Syriac historiographical tradition, see S.A. Harvey, "Remembering Pain: Syriac Historiography and the Separation of the Churches," *Byzantion* 58 (1988): 295–308.

[3] Procopius, *Works*, ed. and trans. H.B. Dewing and G. Downey (Loeb Classical Library; Cambridge: Harvard University Press, repr. 1961) 7 vols. Averil Cameron, *Procopius and the Sixth Century* (Berkeley: University of California Press, 1985) provides the indispensable commentary and critical reassessment, necessary now for all work utilizing Procopius as a source.

[4] Procopius, *History of the Wars*, LCL, vols. 1–5.

artistic adornment, and building efforts of the imperial couple.[5] However, it is his shorter work, the *Anecdota*, or *Secret History*, that has most often captivated western scholars and students alike.[6] Here we have an unparalleled piece of ancient invective, a slander campaign against the imperial couple of staggering scope in a text virtually unique in Byzantine history.[7]

Recent scholarship has stressed a literary approach to the *Anecdota*. An elaborate rhetorical tradition of literary invective lay behind the work, providing stereotypic tropes and character types readily available for discrediting powerful political figures including emperors.[8] Caricatured portraits of "bad" women were standard ploys in such efforts, most often with little or no basis in fact and invariably presented with no interest in the women as figures of any import in their own right. Rather, scandalous depictions of women were stock fare in the character assassination of men. Although a work of unusual scope in its venom as well as its comprehensive assault on Justinian's reign, the *Anecdota* follows the standard conventions of literary invective well-known to every student of ancient rhetoric. As a piece of historical writing it provides an almost wholly fabricated view of Justinian and Theodora, useful as a study in the development of rhetorical method and of dominant cultural themes but offering little substantive information on the imperial couple.[9]

---

[5] Procopius, *Buildings*, LCL, vol. 7.

[6] Procopius, *Anecdota*, LCL, vol. 6.

[7] Cameron, *Procopius*, 49–66 is essential for this material.

[8] Susan Fischler, "Social Stereotypes and Historical Analysis: The Case of the Imperial Women at Rome," in Léonie J. Archer, Susan Fischler and Maria Wyke (eds.), *Women in Ancient Societies: "An Illusion of the Night"* (New York: Routledge, 1994) 115–33; Pauline Allen, "Contemporary Portraits of the Byzantine Empress Theodora (A.D. 527–548)," in Barbara Garlick, Suzanne Dixon and Pauline Allen (eds.), *Stereotypes of Women in Power: Historical Perspectives and Revisionist Views* (Westport, CT: Greenwood Press, 1992) 93–103.

[9] Elizabeth A. Fisher, "Theodora and Antonina in the *Historia Arcana*: History and/or Fiction?" in John Peradotto and J. P. Sullivan (eds.), *Women in the Ancient World: the Arethusa Papers* (Albany: State University of New York Press, 1984) 287–313. Martha Vinson, "The Christianization of Slander: Some Preliminary Observations," in Sarolta Takacs and Claudia Sode (eds.), *Novum Millenium: Festschrift for Paul Speck* (Brookfield, VT:

[6] Nonetheless, it is the *Anecdota* and its particular presentation of Justinian and Theodora that has continued to dominate western imagination.[10] Thus we have an indelibly fixed portrait of Theodora as insatiable in her lust for physical thrills and political power; one whose formative experience in life was a career as child prostitute and sexual acrobat in the circus; whose time as empress was marked by greed, sorcercy, deceit, political intrigue, and wanton disregard for the scruples of any decent, moral human being. In turn, the *Anecdota* presented Justinian as a man measured by his choice of spouse: a driven, demonic soul, consumed by ambition, inhuman in his thirst for power, and enslaved by his unseemly and passionate devotion to his villanous wife. So savage is the portrayal in the *Anecdota* that it is difficult to reconcile how the same author could have produced this work as well as the more sober, formal, and flattering *History of the Wars* and *Buildings*; scholars and students alike have relished the puzzle, with uneven results.[11]

[7] With the help of the ample evidence that survives from other contemporary sources both Greek and Syriac, historians have come to agree that Theodora did manage to rise from the plight of a child actress in Constantinople to find a respectable and quiet life

---

Ashgate Publishing, 1999) provides a fascinating study setting the *Anecdota* into the development of rhetorical traditions of invective as they were adapted and utilized in the Christianized literature of the Byzantine Empire. I am grateful to Prof. Vinson for sharing this article with me prior to its publication.

[10] Cameron, *Procopius*, 67–83 discusses the impact the *Anecdota* has had on the history of scholarship, with a lively presentation of the resulting romanticism and sentimentality. A notable example is Charles Diehl, *Théodora: Impératrice de Byzance* (Paris: E. de Boccard, 1937), where Diehl admits the significance of the Syriac sources but proceeds to follow Procopius' *Anecdota* as a basically credible account. In Browning's *Justinian and Theodora*, the inside dust jacket presents this book as the account of "the peasant's son who became an emperor and the *dissolute actress* whom he placed on the throne beside him... [Justinian] aided—and occasionally frustrated—by his *passionate and unscrupulous consort* [Theodora]" (my emphasis).

[11] At times the authorship of the *Anecdota* has been questioned precisely for this reason. Again, Cameron, *Procopius*, is the essential guide through this historiographical tangle.

in Alexandria in early adulthood. There she seems to have been instructed by such luminaries as the theologian and bishop Severus of Antioch. At some point she met Justinian, then a protegé of Justin's imperial court; thereafter, an imperial edict was passed allowing reformed prostitutes to contract a legal marriage, and further, if granted a high dignity, to marry into the highest rank.[12] Justinian and Theodora were wed in 525 in Constantinople and were devoted to one another through the remainder of their lives. Until Theodora's death in 548, much of their work was undertaken together, as a couple.

[8] Literary sources both critical of and favorable to the imperial couple support this picture, and indicate that Theodora as empress did exercize an unusual degree of authority and influence beyond most who held her position. While the exact authority available to an empress was never clearly defined in Byzantine law, Theodora was able to carve a role for herself that was both traditional (patronage was a respectable activity for a Roman matron, the more so for an empress), and also broader in its effects.[13] Her influence was widely felt, but it is also true that she never attempted to contradict Justinian's policies directly nor to undercut his effectiveness. She remained, then, limited in the power she exercized, but a dominating and impressive personality.[14]

[9] However, the *Chronicle* of Michael the Syrian, written some six centuries after the event, offers an altogether different portrait of Theodora—different both from the painstaking search for historical reconstruction undertaken by modern scholars, and from the scorching pen of Procopius.[15] In Michael's telling, Justinian,

---

[12] *Codex Iustinianus* 5.4.23; cf. D. Daube, "The Marriage of Justinian and Theodora. Legal and Theological Issues," *Catholic University Law Review* 16 (1968): 380–99.

[13] A point stressed by Allen, "Contemporary Portrayals."

[14] An interesting analysis of the primary sources is offered in Charles Pazdernik, "Our Most Pious Consort Given us by God: Dissident Reactions to the Partnership of Justinian and Theodora, AD 525–549," *Classical Antiquity* 13 (1994): 256–81, where Pazdernik considers how the ancient authors depicted the marital relationship between Justinian and Theodora, as a means for resolving the apparent paradox of their conflicting religious loyalties.

[15] J.-B. Chabot (ed. and trans.), *Chronique de Michel le Syrien*, 4 Vols. (Paris, 1899–1905; repr. Bruxelles: Culture et Civilisation, 1963).

while in service to his uncle Justin I, had been on campaign against the Persians in the eastern empire. There, "he came to Mabbug (Hierapolis), and there he took for his wife Theodora, daughter of an Orthodox [= non-Chalcedonian] priest, who, because he was not pleased that she should mix with Chalcedonians was not willing to give his daughter until Justinian made a vow (*aqim qyomo*) that he would not compel her to accept the synod (of Chalcedon)."[16] Subsequently, according to Michael's account, as empress Theodora distinguished herself with concern for the peace of the church, and persuaded Justinian also to work for this. She received the exiled and persecuted Oriental Orthodox in Constantinople, arranging their lodging and provisions, and visiting them constantly. In particular, she patronized the three great patriarchs, Severus of Antioch, Theodosius of Alexandria, and Anthimus of Constantinople, whom she supported in her own palace. She worked quietly and diligently to appease Justinian when the Chalcedonian fanatics roused his passions.[17]

According to Michael, Theodora hid and protected the exiled Oriental Orthodox leaders, but also encouraged the ongoing theological discussions sponsored by her husband.[18] When Justinian's behavior grew increasingly extreme in his opposition to "the believers," to the point of sickness, Theodora secretly summoned the Syriac holy man Z'ura to heal him. Thereafter, Michael says, Justinian did end his excessive use of violence, but did not make peace within the church.[19] When the Chalcedonian patriarch of Alexandria exercized his office with unseemly cruelty, Theodora was able to persuade Justinian to exile him.[20] When Harith bar Gabala, king of the Saracens, requested orthodox missionaries, Theodora sponsored the sending of the Syriac Orthodox bishops Jacob Burd'oyo and Theodore.[21] At her death, Michael claims, Justinian was grief-stricken and gave much gold for

---

[16] Mich. Syr., IX.20; the Syriac text is found in Chabot's edition at 4: 277, center column.
[17] Mich. Syr., IX. 21.
[18] Mich. Syr., IX.22.
[19] Mich. Syr., IX.23.
[20] Mich. Syr., IX. 24.
[21] Mich. Syr., IX.29.

the repose of her soul, while the Oriental Orthodox refused to be demoralized by the loss of their protectress.[22]

[11] For the most part, Michael's account of Theodora as empress accords with sixth century sources, and indeed is heavily drawn from the Syriac writers John of Ephesus and the continuator of the *Chronicle* of Zachariah of Mitylene.[23] This is important, for in the case of John of Ephesus we have a portrayal of Theodora that genuinely rivals Procopius' in length and intimacy of imperial access, but without a trace of the Greek historian's bitter invective. However, Michael has also reworked and reshaped the portrait of Theodora that John and Pseudo-Zachariah provide, as had other Syriac chroniclers between the sixth and twelfth centuries. As we will see, the narrative refashioning of the reign and Theodora's place in it could serve to significantly alter the historical understanding represented.

[12] Yet Michael went further than previous Syriac chroniclers had done, framing his narrative of the reign of Justinian and Theodora with the curious account of Theodora's innocent childhood in the east, raised by a Syriac Orthodox priest who had opposed this marriage unless Theodora's own orthodoxy were guaranteed under oath.[24] While Michael's account appears to be the earliest written source for this story, a variation appears not long after in the

---

[22] Mich. Syr., IX.29–30.

[23] Michael is explicit about his use of John of Ephesus and pseudo-Zachariah. See the discussion and reconstruction of Michael's sources in Chabot, *Chronique*, 1: xxiv–xxxvii.

[24] Unfortunately, Pazdernik, "Our Most Pious Consort," obscures the important issue here of the chronology of the sources, and gives the mistaken impression that the story of Theodora's eastern birth as daughter of a priest might have appeared as early as the ninth century if not even the sixth. At p. 273 n. 71, the *Chronicle of 1234* is misidentified as the *Chronicle of 819*, further supporting this impression. As Jan van Ginkel has argued, it is extremely important to take into account the degree to which later Syriac sources and especially Michael the Syrian have altered the tone and force of material taken from John of Ephesus; see Jan J. van Ginkel, *John of Ephesus: a Monophysite Historian in Sixth-Century Byzantium*, Ph.D. dissertation, Rijksuniversiteit, Groningen (1995), e.g., at 105 and 168. The material from John of Ephesus is treated below.

Chronicle of 1234.[25] In this instance, Theodora's family is from Callinicus rather than Mabbug, and a considerably more romantic tone attends the tale. Not only the child of a Syriac Orthodox priest, Theodora was "a girl of lovely appearance," "adorned with modesty and bodily and spiritual beauty." Justinian heard of her while on military campaign in the east; he fell in love at first sight and begged for her hand. "They [her parents] gave her to him in marriage, except that they were unwilling because he held the doctrine of the Chalcedonians. And he took her with him to the imperial city [Constantinople]. And when he became king, there was much comfort for the [Oriental] Orthodox from her."[26] These two versions of a changed birthright for Theodora attest to a folk tradition circulating among the Syriac Orthodox before Michael's time, but requiring substantial distance from the historical events in question to have emerged in such form.[27] Here was a story befitting the degree of reverence accorded to the "Believing Queen" in Syriac Orthodox tradition, a birthright and family origin well suited to the memory of Theodora as faithful protectress, diligent patron, and profoundly devoted servant of the true church.

---

[25] *Chronicle of 1234*, LIV–LV; in J.-B. Chabot (ed. and trans.), *Chronicon anonymum ad annum Christi 1234 pertinens* (CSCO 81/36, 82/37, and 109/56; Paris, Secrétariat du CSCO, 1916–20; Louvain, Secrétariat du CSCO, 1937); and by A. Abouna and J.-M. Fiey (CSCO 354/154; Louvain, Secrétariat du CSCO, 1974).

[26] *Chronicle of 1234*, LIV; at CSCO 81/36: 192. Later still, Bar Hebraeus mentions the story, following Michael's version as was his wont. Bar Hebraeus, *Chronography*, VIII.78, trans. E.A. Wallis Budge, *Bar Hebraeus, the Chronography* (London: Oxford University Press, 1932) I, 73–4.

[27] It is impossible to ascertain the origins of this story. Chabot himself was baffled, and suggested it originated within the Syriac Orthodox community; *Chronique*, 2: 189 n. 5. It would be wholly out of character for Michael to have invented the story. More likely is its emergence in the folk traditions of the Syriac Orthodox, long before Michael's time. For the scholarly historiographical tradition in which Michael wrote, see J.-M. Fiey, "Les Chroniqueurs syriaques avaient-ils le sens critique?," *Parole de l'Orient* 12 (1984–5): 253–64. I am grateful to Drs. Dorothea Weltecke and Witold Witakowski for their discussions with me on this problem.

The story has been woven into Syriac Orthodox memory to this day.[28]

[13] Scholarly study of Michael the Syrian's *Chronicle* has to date been focused on source critical analysis: who and what were Michael's sources of information for each of the different portions of his *Chronicle*, how faithfully he followed the earlier histories and Chronicles, his "critical" treatment of his sources, and how to account for inconsistencies of chronology. My purpose in this paper is not to examine Michael's presentation of Theodora in terms of its historical veracity. Rather, I am interested in Michael's account as it stands. For this telling of Theodora's story accomplishes a profound re-presentation of the history of the Syriac Orthodox church itself. The memory of Theodora provided Michael a means for remembering the Syriac Orthodox community as it emerged into its own ecclesiastical tradition, for reassessing the separation of the orthodox churches, and for reimagining a tragic if heroic historical experience in terms that validated what that history had become by Michael's day as the churches stood rent by seemingly irrevocable division.[29] In the contrasting portraits of Theodora that survive to us, we can see the contested history of the Oriental Orthodox churches renegotiated in terms of its meaning within the Syriac Orthodox tradition.

[14] For just as Christian historiography used sexual infidelity as a signifier of heresy (or theological faithlessness), so, too, was sexual purity—especially as represented by a female persona—a rhetorical

---

[28] The story of Theodora as the daughter of a Syriac Orthodox priest from Mabbug is commonly known among the Syriac Orthodox today. It is a prominent feature of the play, "Theodora" written in Arabic in 1956 by Mor Faulos Behram, Metropolitan of Baghdad, and translated into Syriac in 1977 by Mor Iuhannon Philoxenos Dolobani, the late Metropolitan of Mardin.

[29] Several papers presented at the Symposium in Commemoration of Mor Michael the Syrian at Ma'arat Saydnaya, Syria, October 1–8, 1999, addressed the situation of the Syriac Orthodox church during Michael's time, both internally and in its relations with other churches. Particularly helpful on this point were: H.E. Metropolitan Mor Gregorios Yohanna Ibrahim, "The Challanges that Confronted the Syriac Orthodox Church of Antioch in the Era of Mor Michael the Great;" and Emma Loosely, "The Crusades: How Were they Perceived in the History of Mor Michael?" See also Chabot, *Chronique*, 1: ii-xvi.

marker for theological orthodoxy.[30] The presentations of Theodora in the accounts by Procopius and Michael the Syrian follow a rhetorical strategy that utilizes her portrayal as the measure of the people with whom she was associated—whether Justinian as an emperor (for Procopius), or the Syriac Orthodox church (for Michael). In both works, Theodora's identity, and especially her sexual identity, become interchangable with the integrity of her community; her "body" stands rhetorically for her "body" of associates—family, spouse, friends, church. In Procopius' telling, she is as faithless and immoral as her husband's reign; in Michael's, she is as chaste and innocent as a church untouched by heresy. In both accounts, her explicitly gendered (and sexualized) portrayal serves as moral marker for the author's own position.[31]

[15] To better understand what Michael has crafted in his presentation of Theodora, we must consider the material on which he drew, as well as the witness of the Syriac chronicles that stood between the sixth century and the twelfth. What portrayal did Syriac chronicles inherit? Was the invective of Procopius efficacious in the historical memory of the east? And why was the memory of Theodora malleable to the point of generating a new

---

[30] Here Christianity follows the inherited rhetorical traditions of classical antiquity. See, e.g., Fischler, "Social Stereotypes and Historical Analysis;" and Averil Cameron, "Virginity as Metaphor: Women and the Rhetoric of Early Christianity," in Averil Cameron (ed.), *History as Text: the Writing of Ancient History* (Chapel Hill: University of North Carolina Press, 1989) 181–205. Cameron's argument is made more extensively in her masterful study *Christianity and the Rhetoric of Empire: the Development of Christian Discourse* (Berkeley: University of California Press, 1991), esp. at pp. 68–72 and 171–80. See also Virginia Burrus, "The Heretical Woman as Symbol in Alexander, Athanasius, Epiphanius and Jerome," *Harvard Theological Review* 84 (1991): 229–48.

[31] Pazdernik, "Our Most Pious Consort," at p. 267 points out that Byzantine historiography tended to associate politically powerful empresses with theologically heterodox movements. For a parallel case from Islamic tradition of conflicting historiographical representations dependent on sexuality and power, see the superb study by D.A. Spellberg, *Politics, Gender, and the Islamic Past: The Legacy of 'A'isha Bint Abi Bakr* (New York: Columbia University Press, 1994). I am grateful to my colleague Prof. Muhammad Qasim Zaman for this reference, and indeed for discussion of the historiographical problems in this paper.

history, a changed history, or indeed a changed quality to the history of Syriac Orthodox memory?

THE SYRIAC SOURCES

[16] One begins, of course, with the complex portrait presented by the sixth century Syriac writer John of Ephesus.[32] John was born early in the sixth century in North Mesopotamia. He was raised in the monastery of Mor John Urtoyo near the city of Amida and subjected in his early adulthood to the persecutions against the Syriac Orthodox that began in 519 under the command of the emperor Justin I. In the course of his travels in exile, John was ordained deacon, then priest for the Oriental Orthodox as they labored to stabilize apart from the Chalcedonian hierarchy. Like many refugees of the persecution, John eventually arrived in Constantinople around 540. Theodora had turned the palace of Hormisdas into a huge monastic complex to house the clergy and monks expelled from their own territories for refusal to comply with the imperial demand for Chalcedonian loyalty, in addition to her work sponsoring other monastic houses. Constantinople was an important gathering place for those opposed to Chalcedon, for Justinian continued to sponsor theological discussions among the divided church leaders and to seek a peaceful reconciliation albeit without any real possibility of compromise. With Theodora's attentive presence, the Oriental Orthodox community could pursue their monastic discipline and further refine their theological acumen while working in the hopes that Justinian would see fit to change his policies.

[17] In Constantinope John became a leader among the exiled community, serving as abbot for many of the Syriac-speaking monastics and spokesman to the imperial court. A frequent visitor to the palace, John became close to both Justinian and Theodora. In 542, Justinian enigmatically chose John to undertake an imperially sponsored campaign of conversion among the pagans and heretics of Asia Minor. A zealous missionary—but certainly

---

[32] S. A. Harvey, *Asceticism and Society in Crisis: John of Ephesus and 'The Lives of the Eastern Saints'* (Berkeley: University of California Press, 1990); for the biographical information on John, see pp. 28–42, 160–5; for discussion of John's portrayal of Theodora, see pp. 80–91, 177–83. Cf. also the important study by van Ginkel, *John of Ephesus*.

not advocating Chalcedonian faith in the process—John led successful missions into the Roman provinces of Asia, Lydia, Caria and Phrygia, returning afterwards to Constantinople where he remained based for the rest of his career. Around 558 he was consecrated titular bishop of Ephesus (a place where he seems never to have resided) by the patriarch Jacob Burd'oyo. Working tirelessly to seek unity amongst the sorely afflicted Oriental Orthodox, and indeed to convince Justinian and then his successor Justin II to seek genuine reconciliation with the opponents of Chalcedon, John labored until his death around the year 589.

In the latter twenty-five years of his life, John wrote the *Lives of the Eastern Saints*, a collection of 58 lives of holy men and women he had met or known well in the course of his travels;[33] and his extensive *Ecclesiastical History* in three parts (the final part written while he was imprisoned under Justin II, and smuggled out in portions).[34] In these two works, we find much information about Justinian and Theodora, and both works were utilized by subsequent chroniclers, including Michael the Syrian. In the case of the *Lives*, most significantly, that information comes in the form of observations of regular behavior and events in the imperial city. In his chapters on the holy ascetics gathered there, Theodora and Justinian are not John's primary focus, but rather enter his chapters just as they seem to have entered into the Palace of Hormisdas in which the exiled resided: with frequent appearances rather than sustained interaction. Hence John gives us a series of "cameo appearances" by the imperial couple while keeping his narrative centered on other people—emperor and empress in the

---

[33] John of Ephesus, *Lives of the Eastern Saints*, ed. and trans. E.W. Brooks, *Patrologia Orientalis* 17–19 (Paris, 1923–5).

[34] John's *Ecclesiastical History* does not survive intact. Parts I and II survive in fragments in the works of later historians, especially the *Chronicle of Zuqnin* (pseudo-Dionysius of Tell-Mahre) and Michael the Syrian's *Chronicle*. Part III, covering the years 571–88/9, is extant complete, and has been edited and translated by E.W. Brooks, *Ioannis Ephesini historiae ecclesiasticae pars tertia* (CSCO 105/54, 106/55; Paris, Secrétariat du CSCO, 1935–6). For further discussion and complete citations of the fragments, see van Ginkel, *John of Ephesus*, 44–85; a more abbreviated treatment is found in Harvey, *Asceticism and Society in Crisis*, 30, 161–2.

background in relation to the "saints" to whom they, like John, were devoted.

In the case of Theodora, John's presentation is particularly complex in its texturing. According to him, long before their actual accession to the throne, Theodora was interceding with Justinian to obtain better conditions for those who suffered under the new policy of persecution against the opponents of Chalcedon. In his account of the two companions Thomas and Stephen,[35] attendants to the bishop Mare of Amida at the time the persecutions first began in 519, John tells us that Stephen was sent to Constantinople to petition on behalf of Mare, whose place of exile in Petra was exceedingly harsh. Arriving at the royal city, Stephen found himself directed "to Theodora who came from the brothel (*porneion*), who was at that time a patrician, but eventually became queen also with king Justinian."[36] Immediately sympathetic, Theodora supplicated her husband, then Master of the Soldiers (John uses the term *stratelates*), that he should intercede with his uncle the emperor Justin I on behalf of the beleaguered bishop, "making this entreaty even with tears." The petition was successful and the bishop with his retinue was able to move to Egypt. But an important pattern had been established, in which Theodora made known her willingness to act on behalf of the opponents of Chalcedon. And indeed, her relationship with Stephen was renewed in successive years, first upon the death of Mare when Stephen returned to ask permission to bury the bishop in his homeland; Theodora, by this time empress, at once issued the order for safe passage and the funeral in his home territory. Later, Theodora herself summoned Stephen by personal letter, "earnestly inviting him to come up to the capital in order to be with her in the palace because of his eloquence and his conversation and his wisdom, and moreover because he also lived a pure life and after the manner of a solitary."[37] Stephen accepted the invitation (apologizing to his companion Thomas that he was only agreeing to go "that this woman's will may not be disappointed"),[38] and for a time resided

---

[35] *Lives*, ch. 13, PO 17: 187–213.
[36] *Lives*, ch. 13, PO 17: 189.
[37] *Lives*, ch. 13, PO 17: 207.
[38] *Lives*, ch. 13, PO 17: 207.

among the gathering Theodora had come to host in Constantinople.

[20] For here was the picture John described: that Theodora turned the "shame" of exile into a glorious experience of Christian witness. Not only did she offer safety in the imperial city for the refugees who gathered there, but further she actively cultivated a holy community of Oriental Orthodox.[39] That is, not only did she welcome whomever among the exiled found their way to the city, but she sought out and personally brought great theologians and church leaders, venerable monastics, renowned ascetics, and wise spiritual counselors. John gives the impression that Theodora had her magistrates combing the provinces, keeping her informed of those with reputations for holiness, for spiritual teachings, for exemplary ascetic devotion. Thus John indicates that many of the faithful arriving in the imperial city were already known to the empress by reputation, and that she received these arrivals not as tattered exiles but as honorable guests of state.[40] The hierarchs, above all, she housed with a formal dignity befitting their ecclesiastical status, even when it was necessary to conceal their whereabouts by stealth.

[21] But consider how John presented the development of this pattern of cultivated relationships and imperial patronage. In his account of Stephen, John had referred plainly but only in passing to Theodora's former life of prostitution.[41] He offered no elaboration, nor judgmental comment (one thinks, by contrast, of Procopius' lascivious pleasure in imagining in great detail Theodora's various tastes, talents, and escapades during those early years of her life). Instead, John clearly assumes her past as a known

---

[39] See the discussion in Harvey, *Asceticism and Society in Crisis*, 86–93, 181–4.

[40] E.g., her reception of Simeon the Persian Debater when he arrived in Constantinople: *Lives*, ch. 10, at PO 17: 157.

[41] J.B. Bury, *History of the Later Roman Empire from the Death of Theodosius I to the Death of Justinian* (London, 1923; repr. New York: Dover Publications, 1958) 2: 28 n. 5, thinks the reference in John of Ephesus to Theodora being "from the brothel" must be an interpolation, but there is absolutely no basis for such a position. As Van Ginkel, *John of Ephesus*, 152 n. 120 points out, the unanimous respect with which Theodora has been regarded in Syriac tradition since the sixth century makes such an interpolation by a Syriac writer most unlikely.

fact that in no way tarnished the integrity of the religious devotion to which she had come. Rather, as Justinian's wife residing in Constantinople as a patrician, Theodora was already known to the opponents of Chalcedon as a faithful friend. In fact, as the extent of Theodora's patronage on behalf of the Oriental Orthodox becomes evident in John's accounts, along with his witness (supported by numerous other sixth century sources, Greek and Syriac alike) of her extensive charitable activities undertaken with Justianian during their imperial reign, one can see the extent to which Theodora was able to represent the power of conversion in her day.[42] From this perspective, her disreputable past mattered only as the measure of how far she had progressed in the Christian life. Thus where her enemies (like Procopius) would use her past to discredit her imperial office and through that Justinian's reign itself, her supporters could see her past as powerful evidence of her strength of conviction: once changed, she had truly repented into a life of faith—a familiar and beloved homiletic and hagiographical theme of the time.[43]

---

[42] Examples of Theodora's deeds on behalf of the Oriental Orthodox, as well as of her charitable activities, may be found in various sixth century sources. E.g., John of Ephesus, *Lives*, ch. 10, PO 17: 157 (correspondence with the Persian Queen; cp. Procopius, *Anecdota*, 2.32–7); *Lives*, ch. 51, PO 19: 161–2 (founding hospitals); Evagrius Scholasticus, *Ecclesiastical History*, 4.10 (her beneficence even for Chalcedonians); ps.-Zachariah Rhetor, *Ecclesiastical History*, VIII.19–20, X.1 (her patronage of the Oriental Orthodox refugees and bishops; her protection of the wronged); John Malalas, *Chronicle*, 17.19 (her patronage of buildings for Antioch, of a jeweled cross for Jerusalem), 18.23–5 (her rescue of girls sold into prostitution by their poor parents, payment to parents, and closing of the brothels); John of Nikiu, *Chronicle*, 93.3 (her eradication of prostitution); Procopius, *Buildings*, I.ii.17 (her patronage of hospices for the poor), I.ix (closing of the brothels and founding a convent for the former prostitutes); John the Lydian, *de Mag.*, III.69 (her sympathy for those suffering injustice).

[43] Hence, John's presentation of Theodora fit a favorite late antique model of female sanctity, that of the penitent harlot. See the illuminating discussion in Lynda L. Coon, *Sacred Fictions: Holy Women and Hagiography in Late Antiquity* (Philadelphia: University of Pennsylvania Press, 1997) 71–94; Benedicta Ward, *Harlots of the Desert: A Study of Repentance in Early Monastic Sources* (Kalamazoo: Cistercian Publications, 1987). The image is a

John presents Theodora's activities on behalf of the Oriental Orthodox both as acts of personal piety and as evidence of her imperial authority. For she did excerize her power as empress in her own right, and not always in conjunction with her husband. When petitioned by Simeon the Persian Debater, John tells us, Theodora "gladly" interceded with the Persian queen on behalf of the orthodox community living somewhat precariously under Persian rule.[44] When Hirith bar Gabala, king of the Saracens, petitioned Theodora about the lack of orthodox priests in the eastern territories because of the devastation of the fierce persecutions suffered there, she immediately gave the orders and the means of passage that led to the consecration of Jacob Burd'oyo and his companion Theodore to serve as bishops replenishing the clergy and hierarchy of the eastern communities with men ordained in Oriental Orthodox faith. Theirs was, John tells us, "active work performed by them during the same persecution, by the instigation and the command of the believing Theodora the queen."[45] John refers to hospitals and other charitable institutions founded by Theodora;[46] he mentions the ceremonial conduct attending her every activity.[47]

John manages to present these deeds as fittingly conducted by the empress: demonstrative of her imperial prerogative, yet not overstepping the bounds of propriety. His careful presentation was not matched by his contemporaries. Procopius, for one, saw Theodora's actions as exceeding what was proper.[48] His critical stance in this regard was not confined to the *Anecdota*. In his account of the Persian War, he describes the consequences of incurring her wrath—a picture confirmed by sources sympathetic to her.[49] His narration of the Nika Revolt in 532, with the famous

---

prime example of the rhetoric of paradox frequently employed by ancient Christian writers; cf. Cameron, *Christianity and the Rhetoric of Empire*, 155–88.

[44] *Lives*, ch. 10, PO 17: 157.
[45] *Lives*, ch. 50, PO 19: 153–8.
[46] *Lives*, ch. 51, PO 19: 161–2.
[47] E.g., as derided by Mare the Solitary, *Lives*, ch. 36, PO 18: 630–3.
[48] A point stressed in Fisher, "Theodora and Antonina."
[49] *Wars* I. xxv. 4–7. The incident here was the downfall of John the Cappadocian; cp. ps.-Zachariah, *Ecclesiastical History*, VIII.14, where the

episode of Theodora's address before the Senate, was clearly not written in admiration of her actions. Rather, the unusual image of a woman's public oratory in the most venerable political setting of the empire provided an unsettling portrayal of Theodora's strength, as well as of Justinian's weakness of character.[50] Even Theodora's supporters shared Procopius' discomfort. Severus of Antioch, known to be a correspondent of the queen even when not residing in Constantinople, grew irritated by what he saw to be her meddling in theological affairs of which she had no real understanding.[51] Certainly, her activity on behalf of the Oriental Orthodox was prodigious, although never such as to bring her into direct confrontation with Justinian.[52] Her patronage of the Oriental Orthodox neither put an end to the persecutions, nor enabled the exiled patriarchs to move about freely; the Palace of Hormisdas functioned in fact as a house prison for the refugees.[53] To some scholars, the circumscribed nature of Theodora's patronage may indicate a real sympathy on Theodora's part with Justinian's goal of ecclesiastical reconciliation, if not an agreement with his methods nor with his own theological views.[54]

John's presentation of Theodora's imperial persona frames his portrayal of her in a certain way. That is, even when referring to his own privileged friendship with the imperial couple, even when presenting her devotional activity, he offers his portrait with a public face, always formal, always respectful of the imperial office itself. Theodora herself is shown to be worthy of that office. Consider again the presentation of Procopius, who claimed in the

---

events are closely connected with the aftermath of the Nika Revolt. *Wars*, I. xxiv.

[50] *Wars*, I. xxiv.

[51] Severus, *Select Letters*, I.63; ed. and trans. in E.W. Brooks, *Athanasius of Nisibis, The Sixth Book of the Select Letters of Severus of Antioch*, 4 vols. (London: Williams and Norgate, 1903). Evagrius Scholasticus, *Ecclesiastical History*, 4.11 mentions letters from Severus to Justinian and Theodora written while the exiled patriarch was in hiding in the east.

[52] L. Duchesne, "Les Protégés de Théodora," *Mélanges d'archéologie et d'histoire* 35 (1915): 57–79, recounts Theodora's involvements in the ecclesiastical crisis of the time.

[53] See the discussion in Harvey, *Asceticism and Society*, 80–93, 177–84.

[54] Cf. Pazdernik, "Our Most Pious Consort;" van Ginkel, *John of Ephesus*, 152–3.

Anecdota to present the "real" Theodora as revealed in her "private" life, dwelling on her own desires and hidden habits, her friendships as sources of surreptitious activitity, her interference in the personal (and sexual) lives of those around her, the "pettiness" of her concerns in contrast to the importance of matters of state.[55]

To appreciate the quality of public respect John offers to Theodora, I take the examples of two direct encounters John describes between the imperial couple and holy men who stood against them. The first occurred when the stylite Z'ura, forced down from his pillar by Chalcedonian persecutors, journeyed to Constantinople in a holy rage to denounce the injustice and impiety of the imperial policies.[56] In an effort to diffuse the storm of the Syrian holy man's arrival in the city, Justinian received him in full assembly in the presence of bishops and senators. Z'ura was not impressed, and with blunt freedom of speech (*parrhesia*) proceded fiercely to upbraid Justinian while instructing him on right doctrine. John reports that it was Justinian who lost control in the situation, falling into a tantrum and shouting insults and invective. Z'ura left, his dignity intact. But Justinian was struck with divine illness, and was soon incapacitated in swollen dilerium. Theodora, "who was very clever," took charge at once, concealing the emperor and sending for Z'ura with urgent supplications that he should come and pray for Justinian, that he might recover and make peace in the church. Z'ura complied, healed Justinian, and took up an aggressive ministry in Constantinople. No more diplomatic in the city than he had been in the palace, the stylite caused such disruption that eventually Theodora was forced to relocate him to safer lodgings in Thrace in order to prevent riots. Meanwhile Justinian had conducted himself in fear of the holy man, curtailing the violence of the persecutions but in the end not changing his policy. In this account, Theodora's strength of character and imposing will are filtered through the lens of her right devotion and piety, presenting strength of will as strength of right faith. It is Justinian who is the volatile, weak-willed, irrational member of the pair, but John's portrayal even here is sympathetic to Justinian as one to a large

---

[55] Especially stressed in Allen, "Contemporary Portrayals."
[56] *Lives*, ch. 2, PO 17: 18–35.

extent imprisoned by his own imperial office in the policies he pursued.[57]

John presented the encounter with Z'ura as a striking affirmation of the holy man's greater spiritual and moral authority in relation to the imperial throne. This authority John saw Theodora appropriately acknowledge, while Justinian wrongly refused to recognize its source in Z'ura's perfect devotion to God. However, John had more difficulty accepting what happened in the second instance, when the holy man Mare the Solitary made his assault on the imperial court following his expulsion from the territory of Amida during the persecutions.[58] Less sophisticated than Z'ura and less dignified in his own conduct, Mare had stormed the court and insulted Justinian and Theodora with such vehement insults that John could not bring himself to describe the encounter, himself too embarrassed to report such treatment of the imperial couple. Here one feels keenly John's devotion to Justinian and Theodora as based both on profound respect for their office but also in a loyalty to their own religious devotion; this encounter clearly caused John a crisis of conscience, for he could not doubt Mare's holiness nor the right cause Mare upheld despite his ill-chosen method. So John writes at some length about the humble response of the imperial couple to Mare—itself evidence of their devotion. Receiving Mare's words in all humility, they offered no rebuke. Instead, Justinian offered his assistance with Mare's ministry in the city and Theodora requested that he join her favored group staying within her palace so that he might provide spiritual instruction for her profit. Mare would have nothing to do with them, setting up his own cell and activity among the poor in the city streets. Theodora frequently sent her messengers with gold to assist his activities—in fact, she hounded him with her attempts

---

[57] John of Ephesus remained unequivocally loyal to emperor and empire throughout his lifetime, enduring the reigns of Justin I, Justinian and Justin II all of whom required active persecution of the non-Chalcedonians. John's loyalty to a political identity in opposition to his own religious convictions is a crucial characteristic of his writing, as demonstrated by van Ginkel, *John of Ephesus*. One result is the unusually humane quality of his criticism for the emperors he served; see Averil Cameron, "Early Byzantine *kaiserkritik*: Two Case Histories," *Byzantine and Modern Greek Studies* 3 (1977): 1–17.

[58] *Lives*, ch. 36, PO 18: 624–41.

at discipleship. For his part Mare refused every such advance as somehow tainted with worldly corruption. When Mare finally died while tending the sick during the bubonic plague that struck Constantinople in 542, John claims that Justinian and Theodora provided a public funeral at their own expense.

The public face John gives to Theodora is not one of unseemly power or interference with governing. Rather, he presents her as always acting with a dignity and piety that were impeccable, and which presented the imperial leadership of the empire as fully worthy of divine favor. John uses the examples of what happened with Z'ura and Mare the Solitary to demonstrate Theodora's perfection in faith in contrast to a more volatile Justinian. When Justinian raged, she calmed him with humility, instructing him to receive the *parrhesia* of the holy men as God's own word. She further saw to it that these monks were provided with means to re-establish their monastic practice and ministry to the needy, and offered public celebration of their holy works. John tells us she often took Justinian with her to visit the "believing community" of holy ascetics, to pray with them and obtain their blessing.[59] She is presented in effect as Justinian's spiritual guide, and in this role resolves the paradox of their divided religious loyalties. In John's eyes, there was not a division of *faith* between emperor and empress: theirs was a shared devotion. The division from John's perspective then lay within Justinian himself, an emperor who truly venerated the Oriental Orthodox yet who instigated and upheld their persecution.

COMPETING MEMORIES

In his presentation of Justinian and Theodora's shared religious devotion, John stands apart from other sixth century sources. Procopius had seen the divided loyalties of the royal couple as a calculated plot to "divide and rule."[60] Moreover, he had presented Theodora's Oriental Orthodox conviction as both politically expedient and an apt choice morally for a person of her "despicable" character.[61] Another Chalcedonian historian of the late sixth century, Evagrius Scholasticus, said it was not clear

---

[59] *Lives*, ch. 37, PO 18: 680; ch. 57, PO 19: 200–6.
[60] *Anecdota*, 10.14–5.
[61] Cp. Vinson, "Sexual Slander."

whether the couple had agreed on their religious policy "because such were their real sentiments... or by mutual understanding."[62] However, in the same passage he offered high praise for Theodora's kindness and munificence towards all her subjects. Indeed, he shared with more sympathetic historians—John Malalas, pseudo-Zachariah Rhetor, and John of Nikiu—a sense of Theodora as Justinian's conscience.[63] Still, all of these writers, in contrast to John of Ephesus, present Theodora as an empress who claimed more power than was seemly for a woman, and whose authority could be willfully and selfishly demonstrated. The particular texturing of John of Ephesus' portrayal, with its emphasis on daily piety and devotional veneration, was of an empress whose orthodoxy was unquestionable. Within the logic of John's portrait, then, it was precisely because of her orthodoxy that Theodora neither counteracted her husband's policies nor abused her office.

Subsequent Syriac chroniclers remember Theodora as protectress of the faithful in the midst of unholy times. The *Chronicle* of Jacob of Edessa notes only her death,[64] while the *Chronicle of 819* states, "In the year Theodora died, Justinian began to persecute Christians over Chalcedon."[65] The complicated relationship of Justinian and Theodora as imperial couple *and* as religiously devoted is left aside. In the ninth century *Chronicle of Zuqnin* (ps.-Dionysius of Tell-Mahre), portions of John of Ephesus' *Ecclesiastical History* are preserved almost intact, especially his account of the persecution against the Oriental Orthodox and Theodora's patronage in its midst.[66] These chronicles, however,

---

[62] Evagrius, *Ecclesiastical History*, 4.10.

[63] Cf., e.g., Ps.-Zachariah, *Ecclesiastical History*, X.1; John Malalas, *Chronicle*, 18.23–4; John of Nikiu, *Chronicle*, 90. 49–51, 87. In the analysis of Pazdernik, "Our Most Pious Consort," these historians use the presentation of Theodora to soften the perceived harshness of Justinian's character.

[64] E.W. Brooks (ed. and trans.), Jacob of Edessa, *Chronicon* (CSCO 5/5 and 6/6; Paris, Secrétariat du CSCO: 1905–7), at 5/5: 321.

[65] *Chronicon anonymum ad annum Christi 819 pertinens* (CSCO 81/36, ed. A. Barsaum; CSCO 109/56, trans. J.-B. Chabot; Paris, Secrétariat du CSCO: 1920–37), at 81/36: 10.

[66] Now available in two fine translations: *Pseudo-Dionysius of Tel-Mahre, Chronicle, Part III*, trans. Witold Witakowski (Liverpool: Liverpool

were produced in a developing historiographical tradition no longer engaged with the Chalcedonian Greek historians of the Byzantine empire; in them no trace of the Greek sources on Justinian and Theodora remain. The portrait John of Ephesus had given, like that of Procopius, had been written in a polemical situation: critics and supporters of Justinian and Theodora alike were presenting the reign. Their accounts were thus offered in a context of varied interpretation and contrasting loyalties. It is that context of multiple presentations that the medieval Syriac chronicles lack when they choose to pass on the memory of Justinian and Theodora.

[30] Thus we arrive at the account by Michael the Syrian. Despite Michael's heavy reliance on John of Ephesus, there is no reference to Theodora's disreputable childhood. Theodora's activities on behalf of the Oriental Orthodox are presented as the mark of her constancy, not as proof of the power of conversion. Moreover, Michael omits John's descriptions of the shared devotional life of the imperial couple and their habitual visits among the "believing saints." He gives a detailed retelling of John's chapter on Z'ura the Stylite. But removed from the context of John's other chapters, it serves to confirm a larger portrait Michael forges, of Justinian as the flawed, headstrong emperor and Theodora as the truly faithful and therefore rational empress. Indeed, in Michael's telling Theodora is a subdued but exemplary empress and wife, for Michael omits accounts or details that gave her the dramatic and dominating persona we find in sixth century sources. Hence Michael shows Theodora to be like the Syriac Orthodox church itself, in a self-presentation Michael offers for his time: faithful child of a faithful priest, one who never strays despite the errancy

---

University Press, 1996); and *The Chronicle of Zuqnin, Parts III and IV, A.D. 488–775*, trans. Amir Harrak (Toronto: Pontifical Institute of Mediaeval Studies, 1999). The Syriac has been edited by J.-B. Chabot, *Incerti auctoris chronicon anonymum pseudo-Dionysianum vulgo dictum*, CSCO 91/43, 104/53 (Louvain, Secrétariat du CSCO, 1927, 1933). As Witold Witakowski has demonstrated, this source tends to preserve John's text more accurately than Michael the Syrian, who abbreviated and otherwise reworked John's material. Some discussion is given in Witakowski, *Part III*, xxiii–xxix; but see also his monograph, *The Syriac Chronicle of Pseudo-Dionysius of Tell-Mahre. A Study in the History of Historiography* (Studia Semitica Upsaliensia 9; Uppsala, 1987).

of her spouse. So, too, has Justinian in Michael's telling become like the Chalcedonian church as seen from Michael's view: stubborn, rash, headstrong—and in fact, misguided.

Michael's portrayal in Book 9 of his *Chronicle* has, I think, refashioned Justinian and Theodora to the likeness of the Chalcedonian and Syriac Orthodox churches, in an identity constructed well after the separation of the churches in the sixth century. For only the clarification of time could have allowed the specific (and ethnic) differentiation of ecclesiastical identity that Michael's portrait assumes. Shorn of their polemical context, the sixth century sources are available for Michael's use in this telling, but with a very different tone than they had when written and thus with a changed content. With the short but crucial addition of a new birthright for Theodora to frame the resulting picture, Michael has truly crafted a new portrait. In his rendering, she is not simply revered among the Syriac Orthodox, but has become their own, a saint of them and for them.

BIBLIOGRAPHY

Allen, Pauline. "Contemporary Portraits of the Byzantine Empress Theodora (A.D. 527–548)." In Garlick, Barbara, Suzanne Dixon and Pauline Allen, eds. *Stereotypes of Women in Power: Historical Perspectives and Revisionist Views*, 93–103. Westport, CT: Greenwood Press, 1992.

Bar Hebraeus, *the Chronography*, ed. and trans. E.A. Wallis Budge. London: Oxford University Press, 1932. 2 vols.

Browning, Robert. *Justinian and Theodora*, rev. ed. London: Thames and Hudson, 1987.

Burrus, Virginia. "The Heretical Woman as Symbol in Alexander, Athanasius, Epiphanius and Jerome." *Harvard Theological Review* 84 (1991): 229–48.

Bury, J.B. *History of the Later Roman Empire from the Death of Theodosius I to the Death of Justinian*. London, 1923; repr. New York: Dover Publications, 1958.

Cameron, Averil. *The Mediterranean World in Late Antiquity, AD 395–600*. New York: Routledge, 1993.

Cameron, Averil. "Early Byzantine *Kaiserkritik*: Two Case Histories." *Byzantine and Modern Greek Studies* 3 (1977): 1–17.

Cameron, Averil. "Virginity as Metaphor: Women and the Rhetoric of Early Christianity." In Cameron, Averil, ed. *History as Text: the Writing of Ancient History*, 181–205. Chapel Hill: University of North Carolina Press, 1989.

Cameron, Averil. *Christianity and the Rhetoric of Empire: the Development of Christian Discourse.* Berkeley: University of California Press, 1991.
Cameron, Averil. *Procopius and the Sixth Century.* Berkeley: University of California Press, 1985.
Chronicon anonymum ad annum Christi 819 pertinens, ed. A. Barsaum, CSCO, 81/36; trans. J.-B. Chabot, CSCO, 109/56. Paris: Secrétariat du CSCO, 1920–37.
Chronicon anonymum ad annum Christi 1234 pertinens, ed. and trans. J.-B. Chabot, CSCO, 81/36, 82/37, and 109/56. Paris: Secrétariat du CSCO, 1916–20; Louvain: Secrétariat du CSCO, 1937; and by A. Abouna and J.-M. Fiey, CSCO, 354/154. Louvain: Secrétariat du CSCO, 1974.
Coon, Lynda L. *Sacred Fictions: Holy Women and Hagiography in Late Antiquity.* Philadelphia: University of Pennsylvania Press, 1997.
Daube, D. "The Marriage of Justinian and Theodora. Legal and Theological Issues." *Catholic University Law Review* 16 (1968): 380–399.
Diehl, Charles. *Théodora: Impératrice de Byzance.* Paris: E. de Boccard, 1937.
Duchesne, L. "Les Protégès de Théodora." *Mélanges d'archéologie et d'histoire* 35 (1915): 57–79.
Fiey, J-M. "Les Chroniqueurs syriaques avaient-ils le sens critique?" *Parole de l'Orient* 12 (1984–5): 253–64.
Fischler, Susan. "Social Stereotypes and Historical Analysis: The Case of the Imperial Women at Rome." In Archer, Léonie J., Susan Fischler and Maria Wyke, eds. *Women in Ancient Societies: 'An Illusion of the Night'*, 115–33. New York: Routledge, 1994.
Fisher, Elizabeth A. "Theodora and Antonina in the *Historia Arcana*: History and/or Fiction?" In Peradotto, John, and J.P. Sullivan, eds. *Women in the Ancient World: the Arethusa Papers*, 287–313. Albany: State University of New York Press, 1984.
Frend, W.H.C. *The Rise of the Monophysite Movement.* Cambridge: Cambridge University Press, corrected ed. 1979.
Harvey, S.A. *Asceticism and Society in Crisis: John of Ephesus and 'The Lives of the Eastern Saints.'* Berkeley: University of California Press, 1990.
Harvey, S.A. "Remembering Pain: Syriac Historiography and the Separation of the Churches." *Byzantion* 58 (1988): 295–308.
Herrin, Judith. *The Formation of Christendom.* Princeton: Princeton University Press, 1987.
Honigmann, E. *Évêques et évêchés monophysites d'Asie antérieure au VIe siècle.* CSCO, 127/Sub. 2. Louvain: Secrétariat du CSCO, 1951.
Jacob of Edessa. *Chronicon*, ed. and trans. E.W. Brooks. CSCO, 5/5 and 6/6. Paris: Secrétariat du CSCO, 1905–7.

John of Ephesus. *Ioannis Ephesini historiae ecclesiasticae pars tertia*, ed. and trans. by E.W. Brooks. CSCO, 105/54, 106/55. Paris: Secrétariat du CSCO, 1935–6.

John of Ephesus, *Lives of the Eastern Saints*, ed. and trans. E.W. Brooks. Patrologia Orientalis, 17–9. Paris, 1923–5.

Michael the Syrian. *Chronique de Michel le Syrien*, ed. and trans. J.-B. Chabot. Paris, 1899–1905; repr. Bruxelles: Culture et Civilisation, 1963. 4 Vols.

Pazdernik, Charles. "Our Most Pious Consort Given us by God: Dissident Reactions to the Partnership of Justinian and Theodora, AD 525–549." *Classical Antiquity* 13 (1994): 256–81.

Procopius, *Works*, ed. and trans. H.B. Dewing and G. Downey. Loeb Classical Library. Cambridge: Harvard University Press, repr. 1961. 7 vols.

Pseudo-Dionysius. *Pseudo-Dionysius of Tel-Mahre, Chronicle, Part III*, trans. Witold Witakowski. Liverpool: Liverpool University Press, 1996.

Pseudo-Dionysius. *Incerti auctoris chronicon anonymum pseudo-Dionysianum vulgo dictum*, ed. and trans. by J.-B. Chabot. CSCO, 91/43, 104/53. Louvain: Secrétariat du CSCO, 1927, 1933.

Severus of Antioch. *Athanasius of Nisibis, The Sixth Book of the Select Letters of Severus of Antioch*, ed. and trans. E.W. Brooks. London: Williams and Norgate, 1903.

Spellberg, D.A. *Politics, Gender, and the Islamic Past: The Legacy of 'A'isha Bint Abi Bakr*. New York: Columbia University Press, 1994.

van Ginkel, Jan J. *John of Ephesus: a Monophysite Historian in Sixth-Century Byzantium*. Groningen: Rijksuniversiteit, 1995.

Van Roey, A. "Les débuts de l'église jacobite." In Grillmeier, A., and H. Bacht, eds. *Das Konzil von Chalkedon: Geschichte und Gegenwart*, vol. 2, 339–60. Würzburg: Echter-Verlag, 1951–4, 1973.

Vinson, Martha. "The Christianization of Slander: Some Preliminary Observations." In Takacs, Sarolta, and Claudia Sode, eds. *Novum Millenium: Festschrift for Paul Speck*. Brookfield, VT: Ashgate Publishing, 1999.

Ward, Benedicta. *Harlots of the Desert: A Study of Repentance in Early Monastic Sources*. Kalamazoo: Cistercian Publications, 1987.

Witakowski, Witold. *The Syriac Chronicle of Pseudo-Dionysius of Tell-Mahre. A Study in the History of Historiography*. Studia Semitica Upsaliensia, 9. Uppsala, 1987.

Zuqnin. *The Chronicle of Zuqnin*, Parts III and IV, A.D. 488–775, trans. Amir Harrak. Toronto: Pontifical Institute of Mediaeval Studies, 1999.